Kaleidoscope Fantasies

Bria "Kalypso" Clark

EST.2020

Bria Kalypso Clark

Kaleidoscope Fantasies

Book One

Bria Clark
The Goddess Kalypso Biz LLC
P.O. Box 13
Reynoldsburg, Ohio, 43086
ISBN 978-1-7336439-8-6

This project is dedicated to those who dream with eyes wide open, to those with a heart as relentless as the ocean, & to those who let their souls sail freely along this journey of life.

Table of Contents

Petals

Petals
Are most beautiful
Wet
Dewy
Dripping rain that fell
From the sky
On the Earth
Soft to the touch
In love with the dirt
Never the same as another
Gentle
Yet strong through the storm
Never gets cold
Petals are warm
I bet they taste sweet
Shine in the Sun
We're flowers in love
Let's let petals run
All over our skin
While we're in the tub
I've got petals for you
Cause you are the one

Sea Sure

I like to think of you as the land
And the sand
On the shore that
My waves wash up on
Earth meeting Water
I'm unsure of you so ...
I don't know whether
To stay
Or to go
Even though you're
Planted firm you also ...
Can get carried away
Sometimes
Just like me ...
I'm not sure what
That means about us
But I love when
The sun shines on us
And we're warm together
I like to leave you little gifts
And I hope that
You miss me when
I'm gone ...

No matter day or night
We're beautiful beside each other
I love how the Moon
Makes me sparkle and shine
And I wonder if you
Adore that about me, too
I love how you
Soak me up
Sometimes this thing we got
It feels like a game
Will she come?
And if she does ...
Will she stay?

Traffic in the Sky

Why can't we all just
Learn to fly?
Too polluted down here
Imagine traffic in the sky
Where we can all breathe
Everything we can see
I would feel closer to God
I would feel closer to me

MOTHEREARTH

I BEND
I DO NOT BREAK
BEAUTIFUL THINGS BLOOM
FROM A BROKEN PLACE
A STRONGER WOMAN
DRAWS POWER FROM HER PAIN
FINDING ONESELF
OVER AND OVER AGAIN
AFTER FORGETTING HER NAME
ALWAYS RISE STRONGER
RETURN TO CONQUER
AND REIGN
SHE REMAINS DIFFERENT
AND REMAINS THE SAME.

Ocean Floor Kisses

I Will
Lie You Down
On The Ocean Floor
And Give Ya
Wet Kisses

The Calm

We would fight so much
In the fire
Even each other sometimes
But our love ...
It is rain
And never fails
To come over us
And cleanse us
Once again.

She is ART

She's a museum full of art
A library full of books
Music that strikes your soul
Her love will have you hooked

Woman Power

You will get lost in her eyes
The juices in your brain will twirl full of thoughts she
whispered in your ear
You will suffer from withdrawal when she isn't near
She will make a man out of you
You will feel no fear
Your world will pause at the sound of her name
Your heart will beat faster, stronger for her
You will be thirsty and hungry for her
Happiness becomes lying in bed
Stroking her head

FEELING

It's so funny how time slows
I'm falling asleep again
There you go ...
Caressing my thighs
Making me feel
A million different ways at one time
Outside and inside
In the front and behind me
It's crazy how you get
Up in my soul and unwind me
See this moment's perfect
Cause ...
I feel like love is paradise
And as I said before
You're caressing my thighs
With one hand, it feels nice
I correspond and grind from behind
The other hand's aggressive
Grabbing my side
I turn around
Those wet lips greet me
Soft plump smooth
My mango starts leaking
Did I say wet?

Cause yes she is
But not as wet as she will be yet
Sounds that escape
Your breath
Make my body scream
"YESSSSSSS"
I'm ready and baby
I love when we're sleepy
In the dark
My boat you row
Gently gently gently
I scream out
And then I cream out
Fucking you
Into a dream
I touch your chest
On your neck
I'm deep breathing
You're pushing inside
The world I forget
I get lost in the vision
Of kaleidoscope sex
Nothing more, nothing less
Transferring energy, releasing stress

DEWY

Your Kisses Taste Just Like Raindrops On The Petals Of
Fresh Flowers In The Springtime
Wet
Wild
Meant To Be

Fountain of Love

I only wish to be the fountain of love from which you
drink ...
Every drop promising eternal passion ...

She Shed

In the dark, I cry alone
The loneliness holds me
Fighting back noise
The silence scolds me
Deep within
The pain ...
It molds me
I'm shedding the skin
That belonged to the old me

Black & White

I'm gonna help you color the parts of yourself that
the world left ...
Black
And White.

OLD SOUL

When an old soul loves you ...
They usually don't believe in the love of a soul
Whose spirit, mind, and emotions
Have travelled many galaxies
Living many lives, knowing all the loves
They normally don't believe in a love
Sent from all around not just from above
They typically don't believe in the love
Of a soul who knows no boundaries
Knowing pains that run deeper than the ocean
They don't believe in love
As mysterious and undiscovered
As the ocean blood in my veins
Mixed with love potions
Heartquake and devotion
They'll never believe that from the cracks
She learned to sew herself together
Indefinitely
They don't believe they're worthy
Of being loved by me
But dearest ...
I love you, definitely.

Ask a Man

I asked a man last night
When was the last time he cried
He thought back for a second
And I wondered why
Men would rather choke on tears
Lock the pain inside
Creating a prison of their fears
Where their happiness hides
A fake wall he put up
Comes tumbling down
Potential love triggers him
And comes around
He lashes out at himself
And hurt them so
Feelings of unworthiness
Ignorance, starts to grow
Another broken person
Created by He
The cycle causes Her
To lose touch with she
She hurts another man
And the funniest thing ...
I fell for that man
So then he hurt me.

Deep Sleep

As I tried
Picturing myself
No longer alive
I cried
I lied on the ocean's sure
Face toward
The sky
Happy to die
Every wave washing over
Took pieces of my soul
Inside
My once heavy soul
It felt oh so
Light
The waves took my body
Under
The ocean and I
Became soul-tied.

Audience

We made love
So beautiful
The world
Stopped
To watch us
To hear us
To fall in love
With us
Even more than
We love each other
There's beauty
In seeing
From the outside
Looking in

I Land

I washed up on the surface
Facedown in the sand
I was this mini island
The island is me
I allowed my roots to travel deep
Into the Earth
I grew up this island
This island is me
Jungle houses
Drums and fire
Building to the beat
Of my heartbeat
This island is me
Love is swinging from
The vines that fall
From the sky
Like eternal rain
From destination to destination
We jump
Like shooting stars
Landing feet in the dirt
Seashells in our hair
Dancing a dance
That sweats raw energy

Vibrating in the air
Love so strong
It's like lava bursts
Vibrant smells
Like honeysuckle hibiscus
Honey and tea
I am the island
The island is me

NAUTICAL NONSENSE

I WANNA SURF THE CURRENTS WITH
SEA TURTLES
AND GIVE SEAHORSES KISSES AFTER
DELIVERY
I WANT TO GO ARM WRESTLE WITH
THE CRABS
AND MAKE MUSIC WITH THE CLAMS
I WANNA WIGGLE MY TAIL WITH
FLOUNDER
AND SEARCH FOR TREASURES IN THE
SANDS
DOWN HERE I RAN INTO
SADE
AND JHENE
DOWN HERE ...
THE WATER BLUE
JUST LIKE KOOL-AID

Dancing in the Rain

If I could be anywhere
RIGHT NOW
I would be dancing
Naked
In the rain
Husband taking cover
Shaking his head
A laugh escaping his teeth
My daughter
Right next to me
I want her to know
What it feels like
To be free
Footprints in the mud
Just like me

Succulent

Sucking on your fingers
Sending chills right up your spine
Nibble on your earlobe
I knew I'd make you mine
While tracing letters on your neck
Tattoos with my tongue
I got the type of pussy
That will make you fall in love
The way I look at you
Like I need direction
But I'm pullin' out that dick
Because it's time for inspection
Feel the outside of my panties
Soakin' wet, clitoris dancing
I got the type of soul
That entrances with romancin'.

ROARING

I heard a roaring in the atmosphere
As I stepped into my divine power
I began to create a path
That truly defined me
A roaring
A whooping and hollering
I heard applause
Rain fell from the sky
I knew they were tears
'Cause my ancestors fight
I heard sirens and horns
Because I had begun
We have got to remember
Just who we come from
Dark history
Can't tell me enough
The truth's in my soul
The truth echoes "ENOUGH"

Paint Me

Paint me how you want me
Am I your thief of a woman in the night
Your gypsy Goddess
Your potential wife?

A shy booky with glasses
Top buns and loafers
Or addicted to music
An escapist, a smoker?

An artist, your doctor
A professional
Your S&M master
Or confessional?

...

Regardless the title
I'm all that in one
Kaleidoscope of a woman
Who let's colors run

My Name is Heartbreak

You feel your heart crumbling in your chest
You cry oceans until your eyes hurt
Light stings, darkness becomes your best frined
You question everyone around you
"How could I ever trust again?"
They knew that power they had
And used it in such an evil way
Thought you had run out of tears
They burst out every single day
Never thought you'd feel this way
But you've truly been broken
Can't make it go away
Can't drive it, can't smoke it
Can't fight it, it's not tangible
The sadness, can't hold it
Nothing is comfort
It's all pain ...
Didn't know how in love you were
Until feeling this way
Standing in the rain
Your name is Heartbreak ...

Raw Diamonds

Do you know the worth of a woman?
Truly?
How does it feel to take off your armor and be
completely naked?
Vulnerable.
When you enter her realm ...
How does it feel to release, sweet
In the heavens between her knees?
How does it feel to look into trustworthy eyes?
How does it feel to know she will not tell the world
your secret?
How does it feel to know she'll stand beside you ...
Against an army that contains the entire world?
How does it feel to know ...
That when you're weak, she'll be strong?
How does it feel to know just the action of lying your
head onto her
Soft, gentle body
Will cleanse you of your doubts and worries
instantly?
How does it feel to know her words are wisdom?
How does it feel to know you are never without?
What you lack, she has in abundance
How does it feel to know ...
She'll love the children she bears you with all her
might?
Do you know what she embodies?
Do you know deep delight?

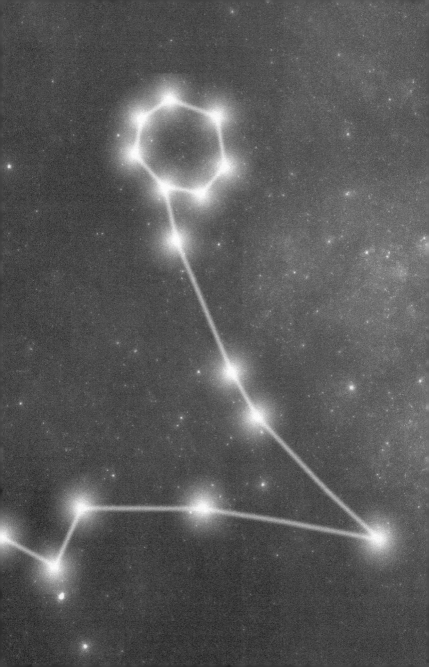

ENCOUNTER WITH THE SCORPIO

Mystery still fills the spaces
In my body and mind
Every time I see you
I'm not sure if it is
Just curiosity
Natural attraction
Or just wild, sexy lust
BUT
We catch each other's eye
A little too often
Sometimes I imagine you there
Remember that time
You showed me your room?
I have no idea how we ended up
On the bed twirling around
You showed your Scorpion tattoo
To this Piscean and
Something inside told me
Fucking around with you

Could be dangerous
And more fulfilling than
We could both imagine
So let's just hold each other
In that beautiful ...
Steamy, uncertain place
Time is never right
But in another realm
Maybe we are aligned
Maybe that's why your
Every presence strikes me
Every time ...

Silk Sheets

Wet sex on silk sheets
Lingerie
Sexy, slip it off 'er
Pedicured toes
Caress the folds
Of the sheets
Like ripples
We so fluid
During foreplay
Would've thought the
Bed was water
Rain sounds
In the background
And your breathing
Makes me hotter

ThrillHer

She's no temporary thrill
She's the roller coaster
You'll never want to stop enjoying the ride.

Years and years in
You still get shy
Nights after dates, still chills up your spine.

She'll make the hairs on the back of your neck
Stand up
With not one touch.

Kalypso in Wonderland

The clock on my nightstand
Tick tick ticks away
As my eyes slowly shut
And I fall deep, deep
Down the rabbit's hole
Layers and layers
Of "What's passing by?"
Realms and worlds
Colors, auras, energies
I am shifting, experiencing
And changing and watching
And falling and falling
And falling and falling
I feel it in my mind
And physically
Just where am I going?
Nothing to grab hold of
No destination below
Or above me
I don't feel scared
I am excited and curious
Because I have no
Fucking idea what comes next

But the fact I'm here
Experiencing this
Feels so damn good
The only thing I know
Is that I am alive
I am here inside of this body
And you know what?
I'm not sure what happens
After I fall into this trance
Or where it is that I go
But I always wake up
The next morning
No memories
Ready for a new world
Earthling say "HELLO".

WildStyle

Smellin' wild good
Lick the outside of my panties
Sex so nasty hot drippy and fancy
Futuristic pussy
Got ya dick dancin'
Janet J throbbin'
Squirtin' and sextin'
I desire to light ya
Soul on fire
Fuck weed, baby
I can take you higher
Moaning in ya ear
Choke me up
"Shut up"
Let it go, baby
I can get it back up
Grippin' while you in it
Grindin' right back
Pretty Ricky body
Yeah, I got it like that ...
winks

BREATHE

I thought I was just
A breath of fresh air
But in reality ...
I'm a wave of electric energy
I will seep through you
Make you light
And excited
There are all the things
To be happy about
In this world.

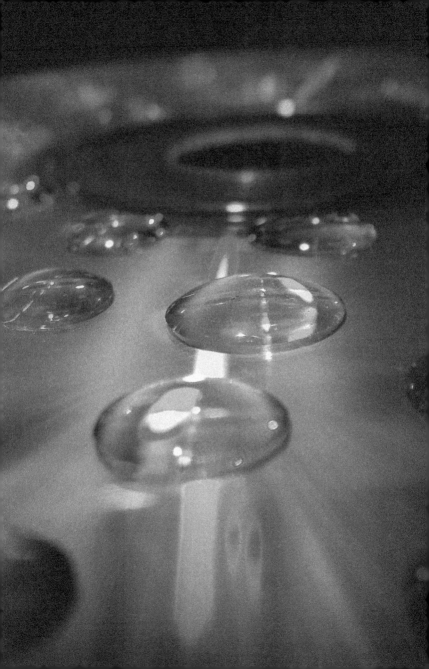

Just like MUSE-ic

She Erykah Badu thick
Jhene Aiko wet
J.Cole minded
Nasty like Keith Sweat
She sound like ocean waves
Could've called her Sade
Love how she speak her mind
Like a female Wale.

About the Author

Bria "The Goddess Kalypso" Clark was born and raised in Columbus, Ohio in 1994. She is described as a multifaceted, multidemensional, spiritual, expressive, and creative woman. An experienced venturer throughout many journeys in life, this woman truly marches to the beat of her own drum. A twinkle in her eye, you can never truly grasp all the ideas swimming in her head. At 26 years of age, she is ready to embark on her journey as an artist, author, clothing designer, and business owner. A graduate of Columbus Africentric Early College (2012), Bria is proud to say this is where she acquired her roots in African heritage, traditions, morals, and values. It is important to her that she applies the wisdom gained from every experience encountered. Bria later attended two HBCUs, Wilberforce University and Bethune Cookman College for business. Bria is a college dropout and decided against paying more money for college to embark on a separate journey, fueled by the desire to create her own path from scratch with no regrets.

"Kaleidoscope Fantasies" is the very first book of a series of poetry written organically. This particular book contains a wide variety of free verse poetry. It is sensual, imaginative, extraordinary, and watery. This author wants the world to know they are diving into the mind of a woman who promotes self-love and healing, as well as the mind of a woman that wants to leave a legacy behind. Allow this kaleidoscope of fantasies to inspire you to dream with eyes wide open, relate, and be filled with "vibez".

<u>Social Media</u>

Instagram:
@thegoddesskalypso

Facebook:The Goddess
Kalypso Biz

Snapchat
@kalypso.bri

Twitter:
@kalypsogoddess

Thank YOU for diving in!

CPSIA information can be obtained
at www.ICGtesting.com
Printed in the USA
LVHW012317210221
679514LV00006B/581

9 781733 643986